CAT STEVENS
GREATEST HITS

Order No. AM 71208
International Standard Book Number: 0.8256.1196.2

Exclusive Distributors:
Music Sales Corporation
257 Park Avenue South, New York, NY 10010
Music Sales Limited
8/9 Frith Street, London W1V 5TZ England
Music Sales Pty. Limited
120 Rothschild Street, Rosebery, Sydney, NSW 2018, Australia

Printed in the United States of America by
Vicks Lithograph and Printing Corporation

PEACE TRAIN

Words and Music by
CAT STEVENS

8

9

10

ANOTHER SATURDAY NIGHT

Words and Music by
SAM COOKE

CAN'T KEEP IT IN

Words and Music by
CAT STEVENS

18

WILD WORLD

Words and Music by
CAT STEVENS

SITTING

Words and Music by
CAT STEVENS

1.2. Oh I'm on my way I know___ I am some - where not so far from here.___
But times___ there were when I thought not___
some - where not so far from here.___

and keep on won-d'ring if I sleep too long,—
and if I make it to the wat - er - side,—

will I e - ven wake up a - gain _____ or some - thing.
I'll be sure to write you a note ——

— or some-thing.

Coda

— Up where you start - ed from, —— you're gon-na wind —— up where you start - ed from.

(Spoken)

READY

Words and Music by
CAT STEVENS

33

FATHER & SON

Words and Music by
CAT STEVENS

HARD HEADED WOMAN

Words and Music by
CAT STEVENS

MOONSHADOW

Words and Music by
CAT STEVENS

I won't have to work no ___ more, and
I won't have to cry no ___ more, yes

I'm be-in' fol-lowed by a moon shad-ow, moon shad-ow, moon shad-ow, ___

leap-in' and hop - in' on a moon shad-ow, moon shad-ow. moon shad-ow. ___ and

if I ev - er lose ___ my legs. ___ I won't moan ___ and
if I ev - er lose ___ my mouth. ___ or my teeth ___

45

OH VERY YOUNG

Words and Music by
CAT STEVENS

Oh ve-ry young what will you leave us this time___ you're on-ly

dan-cing on___ this earth for a short while___ and though your dreams may toss and turn you now___

they will van-ish a-way___ like your Dad's_ best jeans___ de-nim blue_

MORNING HAS BROKEN

Words by ELEANOR FARJEON
Musical Adaptation by CAT STEVENS

1.4. Morn - ing has brok - en   like the first   morn -
2. Sweet the rain's new   fall,   sun - lit from   heav -

3. Mine is the sun - light, Mine is the morn -

ing, Born of the one light E - den saw play.

Praise with e - la - tion, Praise ev-'ry morn -

ing, God's re - cre - a - tion of the new day.

54

FATHER & SON

Words and Music by Cat Stevens

It's not time to make a change just relax take it easy,
You're still young that's your fault there's so much you have to know
Find a girl settle down if you want you can marry,
Look at me I am old but I'm happy,
I was once like you are now and I know that it's not easy to be calm
When you've found something going on,
But take your time think a lot, think of ev'rything you've got
For you will still be here tomorrow but your dreams may not.
How can I try to explain?
When I do he turns away again,
It's always been the same, same old story,
From the moment I could talk I was ordered to listen
Now there's a way and I know that I have to go away,
I know I have to go. It's not time to make a change
Just sit down take it slowly, you're still young
That's your fault there's so much you have to go through.
Find a girl settle down if you want you can marry,
Look at me I am old but I'm happy,
All the times that I've cried keepin', all the things I knew inside
It's hard but it's harder to ignore it.
If they were right I'd agree but it's them they know not me,
Now there's a way and I know that I have to go away,
I know I have to go.

HARD HEADED WOMAN

Words and Music by Cat Stevens

I'm looking for a hard headed woman,
Ohe who'll take me for myself,
And if I find my hard headed woman
I won't need noboby else, no, no, no.
I'm looking for a hard headed woman
One who'll make me do my best,
And if I find my hard headed woman
I know the rest of my life will be blessed, yes, yes, yes.
I know a lot of fancy dancers
People who can glide you on a floor,
They move so smooth but have no answers
When you ask why'd you come here for?
Why? (I don't know)
I know many fine feathered friends
But their friendliness depends on how you do.
They know many sure fired ways to find out
The one who pays and how you do.
I'm looking for a hard headed woman,
One who will make me feel so good,
And if I find my hard headed woman
I know my life will be as it should, yes, yes, yes.
I'm looking for a hard headed woman
One who'll make me do my best,
And if I find my hard headed woman.

READY

Words and Music by Cat Stevens

I love, I love I'm ready to love yes
I love, I love I'm ready to love yeah
I love, I love I'm ready to ready to ready to love
I love, I love I'm ready to love yeah,
You keep me awake with your white lilly smile
Don't keep me watching your charms all the while
'Cause as all the wise men say grab it if it comes your way
I'm ready oh I love, I love I'm ready to love yeah
Ready to love, I love, I love I'm ready to love yeah
You make me feel things I've never felt before
Help me baby eyes and open up the door
You make me real to ev'ryone and ev'ry day
I, I thank the lord, that you came along this way
It's no more an illusion that I can say
I love, I love I'm ready to love yeah.
I love, I love I'm ready to love yes
I love, I love I'm ready, ready, ready, ready to love
I love, I love I'm ready to love oo. I love I love I'm ready,
Ready to love ready to love, I love, I love I'm ready, ready to love.

SITTING

Words and Music by Cat Stevens

Oh I'm on my way I know I am somewhere not so far from here.
All I know is all I feel right now.
I feel the power growing in my hair,
Sitting on my own not by myself, ev'rybody's here with me.
I don't need to touch your face to know,
And I don't need to use my eyes to see.
I keep on wond'ring if I sleep too long,
Will I always wake up the same (or so)
And keep on wond'ring if I sleep too long,
Will I even wake up again or something.
Oh I'm on my way I know I am
But times there were when I thought not
Bleeding half my soul in bad company.
I thank the moon I had the strength to stop.
Now I'm not making love to anyone's wishes,
Only for that light I see,
'Cause when I'm dead and lowered in my grave,
There's gonna be the only thing that's left of me.
And if I make it to the waterside,
Will I even find me a boat (or so)
And if I make it to the waterside,
I'll be sure to write you a note or something.
Oh I'm on my way I know I am somewhere not so far from here.
All I know is all I feel right now.
I feel the power growing in my hair,
Oh life is like a maze of doors
And they all open from the side you're on.
Just keep on pushing hard, boy.
Try as you may, you're gonna wind up where you started from,
You're gonna wind up where you started from.

OH VERY YOUNG

Words and Music by Cat Stevens

Oh very young what will you leave us this time
You're only dancing on this earth for a short while
And though your dreams may toss and turn you now
They will vanish away like your Dad's best jeans
Denim blue fading up to the sky
And though you want him to last forever
You know he never will, you know he never will,
And the patches make the goodbye harder still.
Oh very young what will you leave us this time
There'll never be a better chance to change your mind
And if you want this world to see a better day
Will you carry the words of love with you
Will you ride the great white bird into heaven
And though you want to last forever you know you never will
You know you never will, and the goodbye makes the journery harder still
Will you carry the words of love with you, will you ride
Oh, oh very young what will you leave us this time
You're only dancing on this earth for a short while
Oh very young what will you leave us this time.

PEACE TRAIN

Words and Music by Cat Stevens

Now I've been happy lately thinkin' about the good things to come,
And I believe it could be. Something good has begun.
Oh, I've been smilin' lately dreamin' about the world as one,
And I believe it could be. Someday it's goin' to come.
'Cause out on the edge of darkness there rides a peace train.
Oh, peace train take this country,
Come take me home again.
Now I've been smilin' lately thinkin' about the good things to come,
And I believe it could be. Something good has begun.
Oh, peace train soundin' louder, glide on the peace train.
Come on the peace train. Peace train holy roller,
Ev'ryone jump up on the peace train.
Come on now peace train.
Get your bags together go bring your good friends too.
Because it's gettin' nearer, it soon will be with you.
Oh come and join the living it's not so far from you.
And it's gettin' nearer soon it will all be true.
Oh peace train sounding louder
Glide on the peace train, oo come on now peace train, peace train.
Now I've been cryin' lately thinkin' about the world as it is
Why must we go on hating, why can't we live in bliss.
'Cause out on the edge of darkness there rides a peace train
Oh peace train take this country, come take me home again.
Oh peace train soundin' louder, glide on the peace train.
Come on the peace train. Peace train holy roller,
Ev'ryone jump up on the peace train.
Come on now peace train.
Come on peace train. Yes it's the peace train!

MOONSHADOW

Words and Music by Cat Stevens

Oh I'm bein' followed by a moon shadow,
Moon shadow, moon shadow,
Leapin' and hopin' on a moon shadow, moon shadow,
Moon shadow, and if I ever lose my hands,
Lose my plough, lose my land, oh if I ever lose my hands,
Oh if I won't have to work no more, and if I ever lose my eyes,
If my colour all runs dry, yes if I ever lose my eyes,
Oh if I won't have to cry no more,
Yes I'm bein' followed by a moon shadow,
Moon shadow, moon shadow, leapin' and hopin' on a moon shadow,
Moon shadow, moon shadow, and if I ever lose my legs,
I won't moan and I won't beg, yes if I ever lose my mouth,
Oh if I won't have to walk any more and if I ever lose my mouth,
Or my teeth north or south, yes if I ever lose my mouth,
Oh if I won't have to talk. Did it take long to find me?
I asked the faithful light. Did it take long to find me
And are you gonna stay the night.
Oh I'm bein' followed by a moon shadow, moon shadow,
Moon shadow, leapin' and hopin' on a moon shadow,
Moon shadow, moon shadow, moon shadow, moon shadow,
Moon shadow, moon shadow.

ANOTHER SATURDAY NIGHT

Words and Music by Sam Cooke

Another Saturday night and I ain't got nobody,
I've got some money 'cause I just got paid;
Now how I wish I had someone to talk to, I'm in an awful way.
I got in town a month ago, I seen a lot of girls since then,
If I could meet 'em I could get 'em but as yet I haven't met 'em
That's how I'm in the state I'm in.
Oh another Saturday night and I ain't got nobody,
I've got some money 'cause I just got paid;
Now how I wish I had someone to talk to, I'm in an awful way.
Another fella told me he had a sister who looked just fine
Instead of bein' my deliv'rance she had a strange resemblance to a cat
Name Frankenstein. Ooh la. Another Saturday night and I ain't got nobody,
I've got some money 'cause I just got paid;
Now how I wish I had someone to talk to, I'm in an awful way.
It's hard on a fella when he don't know his way around
If I don't find me a honey to help me spend my money
I'm gonna have to blow this town. Oh no
Oh no another Saturday night and I ain't got nobody,
I've got some money 'cause I just got paid;
Now how I wish I had someone to talk to, I'm in an awful way.
Another Saturday night and I ain't got nobody,
I got some money 'cause I just got paid;
How I wish I had someone to talk to, I'm in an awful,
Ooh, I'm in an awful way, he's in an awful way,
I'm in an awful way, I'm in an awful way, he's in an awful way.

MORNING HAS BROKEN

Words by Eleanor Farjeon
Musical arrangement by Cat Stevens

Morning has broken like the first morning,
Blackbird has spoken like the first bird.
Praise for the singing, praise for the morning,
Praise for them springing fresh from the world.
Sweet the rain's new fall,
Sunlit from heaven, like the first dew fall on the first grass.
Praise for the sweetness of the wet garden,
Sprung in completeness where his feet pass.
Mine is the sunlight, mine is the morning
Born of the one light Eden saw play.
Praise with elation, praise ev'ry morning,
God's recreation of the new day.
Morning has broken like the first morning,
Blackbird has spoken like the first bird.
Praise for the singing, praise for the morning,
Praise for them springing fresh from the world.

CAN'T KEEP IT IN

Words and Music by Cat Stevens

Oh I can't keep it in, I can't keep it in,
I've gotta let it out. I've got to show the world,
World's gotta see, see all the love, love that's in me.
I said, why walk alone, why worry when it's warm over here.
You've got so much to say, say what you mean,
Mean what you're thinking and think anything.
Oh why, why must you waste your life away,
You've got to live for today, then let it go.
I want to spend this time with you,
There's nothing I wouldn't do if you let me know.
And I can't keep it in, I can't hide it and I can't lock it away.
I'm up for your love, love heats my blood,
Blood spins my head and my head falls in love, oh.
No I can't keep it in, I can't keep it in, I've gotta let it out.
I've gotta show the world, world's gotta know,
Know of the love, love that lies low, so why can't you say,
If you know then why can't you say.
You've got too much deceit, deceit kills the light,
Light needs to shine, I said shine light, shine light, love.
That's no way to live your life, you allow too much to go by,
And that'won't do, no lover.
I want to have you here by my side, now don't you run,
Don't you hide while I'm with you, 'n' I can't keep it in,
I can't keep it in, I've gotta let it out.
I've got to show the world, world's gotta see, see all the love,
Love that's in me. I said, why walk alone, why worry when it's warm over here.
You've got so much to say, say what you mean, mean what you're thinking
And think anything, why not? Now why, why, why not.

WILD WORLD

Words and music by Cat Stevens

Now that I've lost ev'rything to you
You say you wanna start something new and
It's breaking my heart you're leaving.
Baby, I'm grievin'!
But if you want to leave take good care,
Hope you have a lot of nice things to wear
But then a lot of nice things turn bad out there.
Oh baby, baby it's a wild world.
It's hard to get by just upon a smile.
Oh, baby, baby it's a wild world.
I'll always remember you like a child, girl.
You know I've seen a lot of what the world can do
And it's breaking my heart in two
Because I never want to see you sad, girl.
Don't be a bad girl.
But if you want to leave take good care,
Hope you make a lot of nice friends out there
But just remember there's a lot of bad and beware.
Oh baby, baby it's a wild world.
It's hard to get by just upon a smile.
Oh, baby, baby it's a wild world.
I'll always remember you like a child, girl.
Baby I love you,
But if you want to leave take good care,
Hope you make a lot of nice friends out there.
But just remember there's a lot of bad and beware.
Oh baby, baby it's a wild world.
It's hard to get by just upon a smile.
Oh, baby, baby it's a wild world,
I'll always remember you like a child, girl.